SUPER EASY CHRISTMAS M
SHEET MUSIC FOR BEGI

BY KIRK TATNALL

ISBN: 9798854693769

HOW TO GET THE AUDIO

The free audio files for this book are available to download or stream at: *troynelsonmusic.com.*

We are available to help you with your audio downloads and any other questions you may have. Simply email *help@troynelsonmusic.com.*

See below for the recommended ways to listen to the audio:

Download Audio Files	Stream Audio Files
• Download Audio Files (Zipped)	• Recommended for CELL PHONES & TABLETS
• Recommended for COMPUTERS on WiFi	• Bookmark this page
• A ZIP file will automatically download to the default "downloads" folder on your computer	• Simply tap the PLAY button on the track you want to listen to
• Recommended: download to a desktop/laptop computer *first*, then transfer to a tablet or cell phone	• Files also available for streaming or download at: *soundcloud.com/troynelsonbooks*
• Phones & tablets may need an "unzipping" app such as iZip, Unrar, or Winzip	
• Download on WiFi for faster download speeds	

**To download the companion audio files for this book,
visit:** troynelsonmusic.com/audio-downloads/

INTRODUCTION

Welcome to *Super Easy Christmas Mandolin Sheet Music for Beginners*! This collection of timeless songs is designed to help beginning mandolin players of all ages learn Christmas carols quickly and easily. In this book, you'll find easy-to-follow arrangements of classic holiday songs, complete with lyrics, chord charts, strum patterns, and mandolin tab. Each song has been carefully selected for holiday fun and is presented in a way that is easy to understand and play.

What differentiates this book from other mandolin songbooks? Glad you asked. The most notable differences are:

- **Music Size:** The staffs and notes are enlarged so the music is easier to read.

- **Note Names:** The names of the notes are clearly displayed inside extra-large note heads.

- **Mandolin Tab:** Tab notation ensures that you'll find the correct note. In tab, each line represents a string. The bottom line is string 4 (G, closest to the ceiling) and the top line is string 1 (E, closest to the floor.) A number placed on a line indicates the fret and string on which the note is played, respectively. For example, a "3" on the top line indicates that you play fret 3, string 1, and a "0" on the third line means you play string 3 open (no fingers).

- **Chord Charts:** The chords for each song are provided above the staff. If you'd like to add them to the arrangement, simply use the chord charts and strum along (strum patterns are provided in the bottom tab staff).

- **Three Ways To Play:** Learn the melody on your mandolin (top tab staff), strum the chords (bottom tab staff), or strum the chords and sing the melody.

- **Key Signatures:** Key signatures are included but accidentals (sharps, flats, and naturals) have been provided in the arrangements for ease of use. Some pieces have been arranged in keys that are different from the original compositions to make them easier to play.

- **Audio Tracks:** Listen to the corresponding audio track to get a feel for the song before you play it. Individual tracks are provided for the melody and stum pattern, as well as one with the melody and strumming combined.

THE BASICS

THE MUSIC ALPHABET

The letters of the music alphabet are:

A B C D E F G

These letters are assigned to notes on a staff consisting of five lines and four spaces. The notes that appear on the lines are:

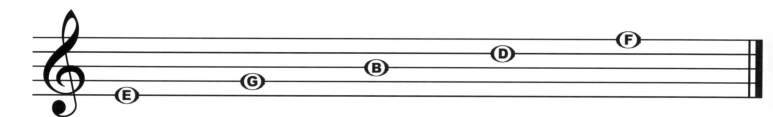

An easy way to memorize these five notes is to use a phrase in which each word begins with the letter on the staff:

<u>E</u>very <u>G</u>ood <u>B</u>oy <u>D</u>oes <u>F</u>ine

The notes that appear in the four spaces are:

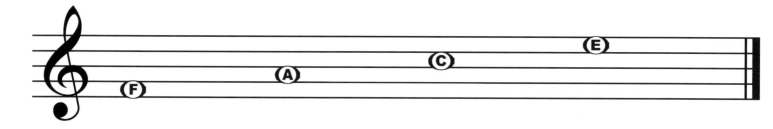

You may have noticed that these four notes, from bottom to top, spell the word **F A C E**, which makes them easy to remember.

Notes that appear *above* or *below* the staff require a *ledger line*, which is a short line that extends the range of the staff.

4

TIME SIGNATURE

The *time signature* consists of two numbers. For the purpose of this book, we'll focus on the top number, which indicates how many beats are in a *measure*, the space between the vertical lines along the staff.

Three Beats

3
4

Four Beats

4
4

ACCIDENTALS

Some notes fall between the letters of the musical alphabet. When this happens, we use an *accidental*. Here are the three types of accidentals:

Sharp Sign

♯

Flat Sign

♭

Natural Sign

♮

A sharp sign *raises* the pitch of a note by a half step, or one fret on the ukulele. A flat sign *lowers* the pitch by a half step. A natural sign cancels the sharp or flat.

RHYTHM PRIMER

Playing the right note is only half the equation when playing songs; you also have to know *when* to play them and for *how long*. This is rhythm. Here are the most common rhythms you'll play in this book:

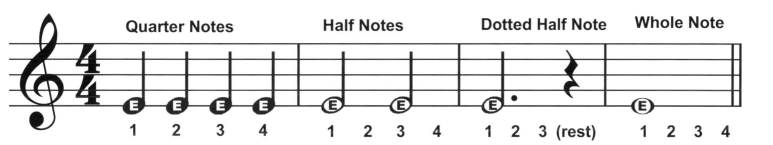

ANGELS FROM THE REALMS OF GLORY

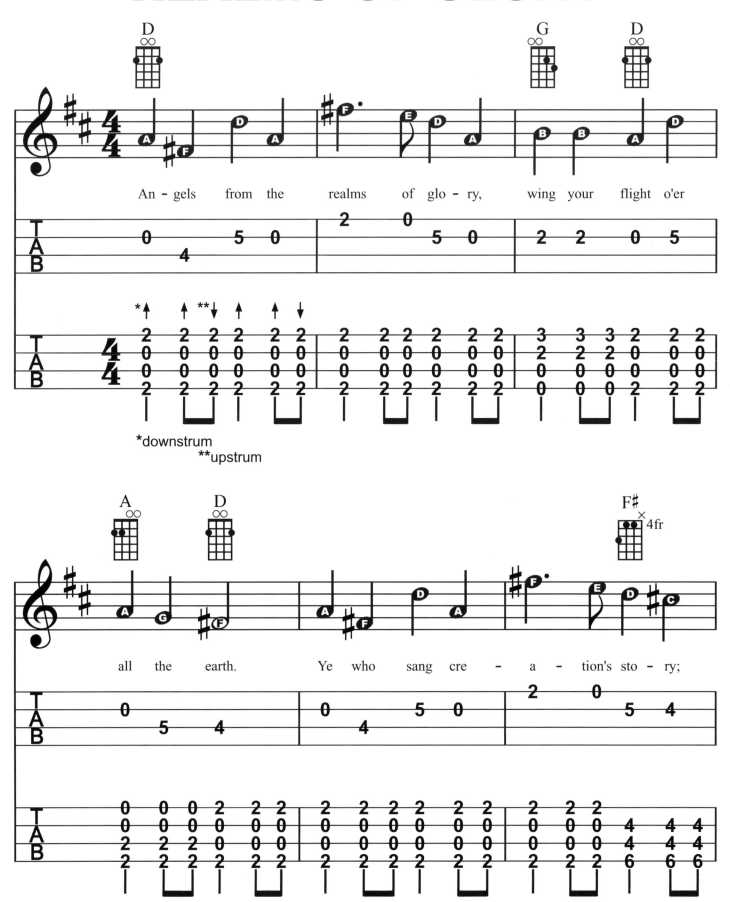

*downstrum
**upstrum

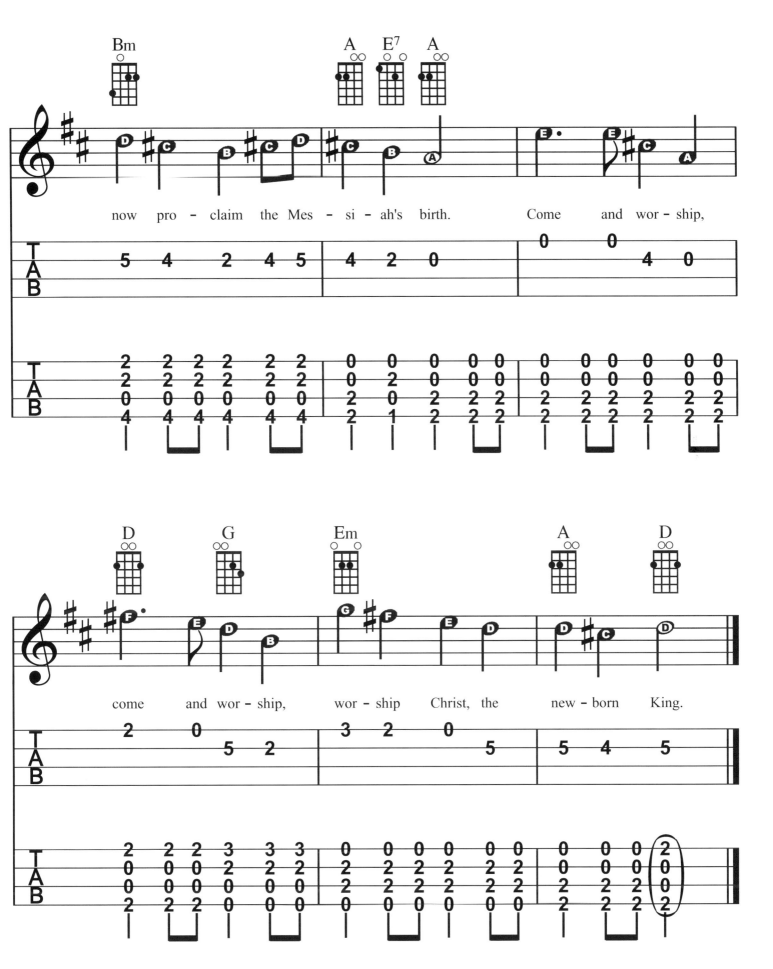

ANGELS WE HAVE HEARD ON HIGH

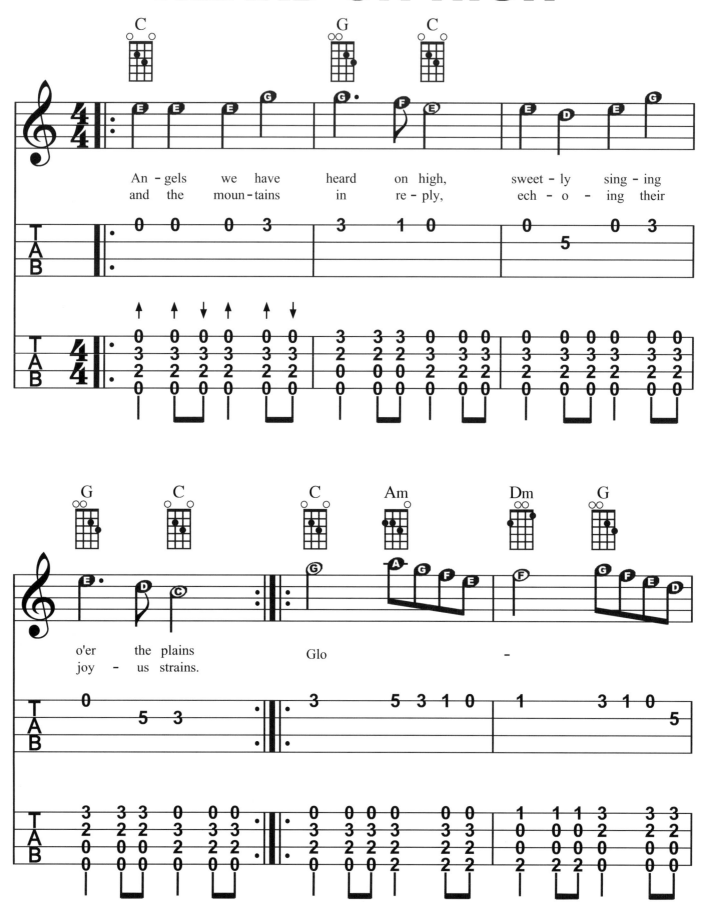

An - gels we have heard on high, sweet - ly sing - ing
and the moun - tains heard in re - ply, ech - o - - ing their

o'er the plains
joy - us strains.

Glo - -

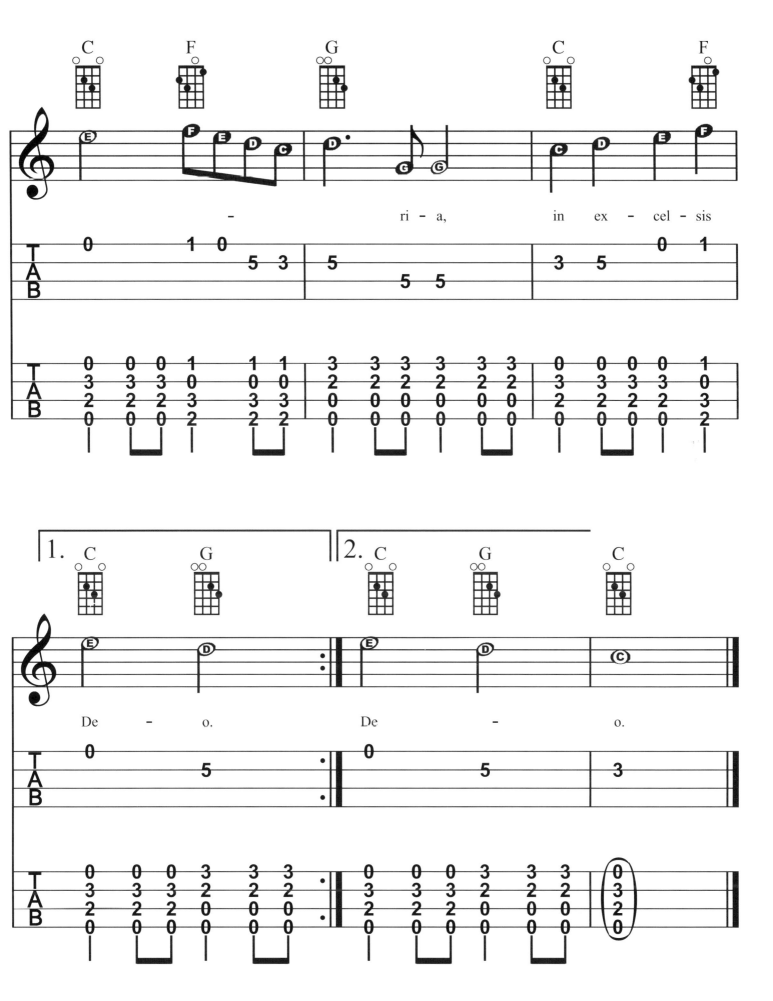

AULD LANG SYNE

AWAY IN A MANGER

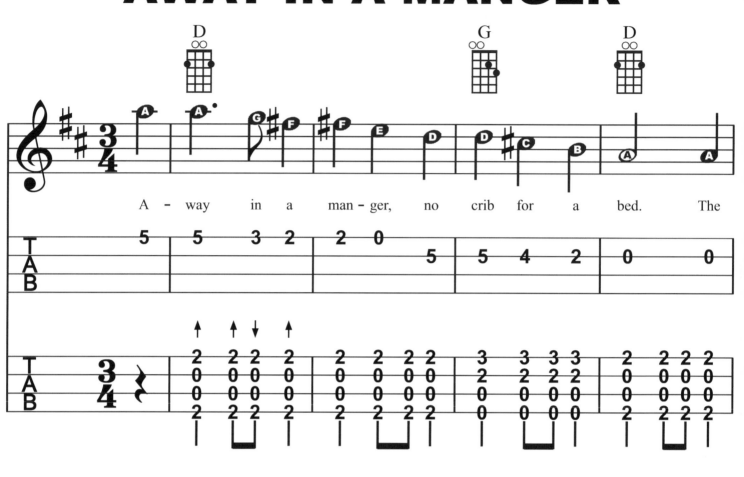

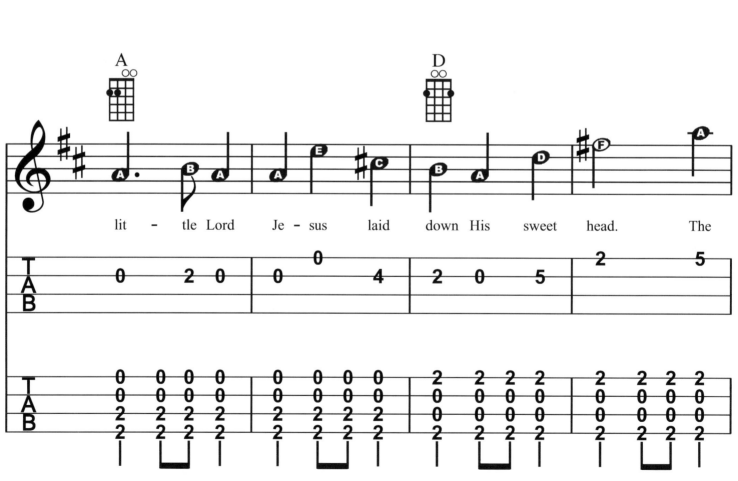

DECK THE HALLS

Deck the halls with boughs of hol - ly,

fa - la - la - la - la, la la - la - la.

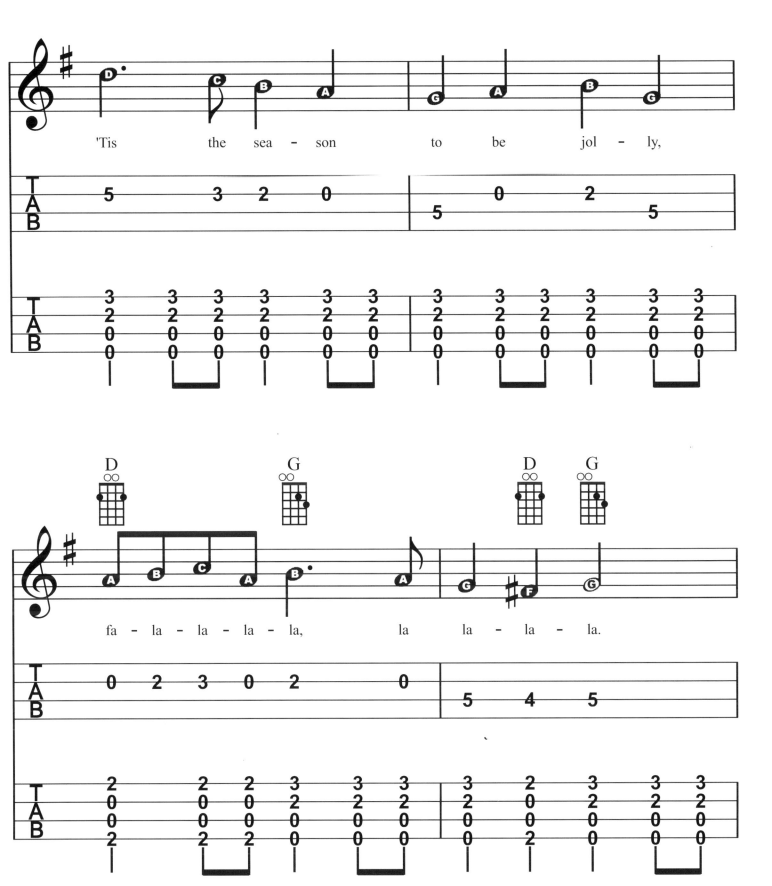

'Tis the sea - son to be jol - ly,

fa - la - la - la - la, la la - la - la.

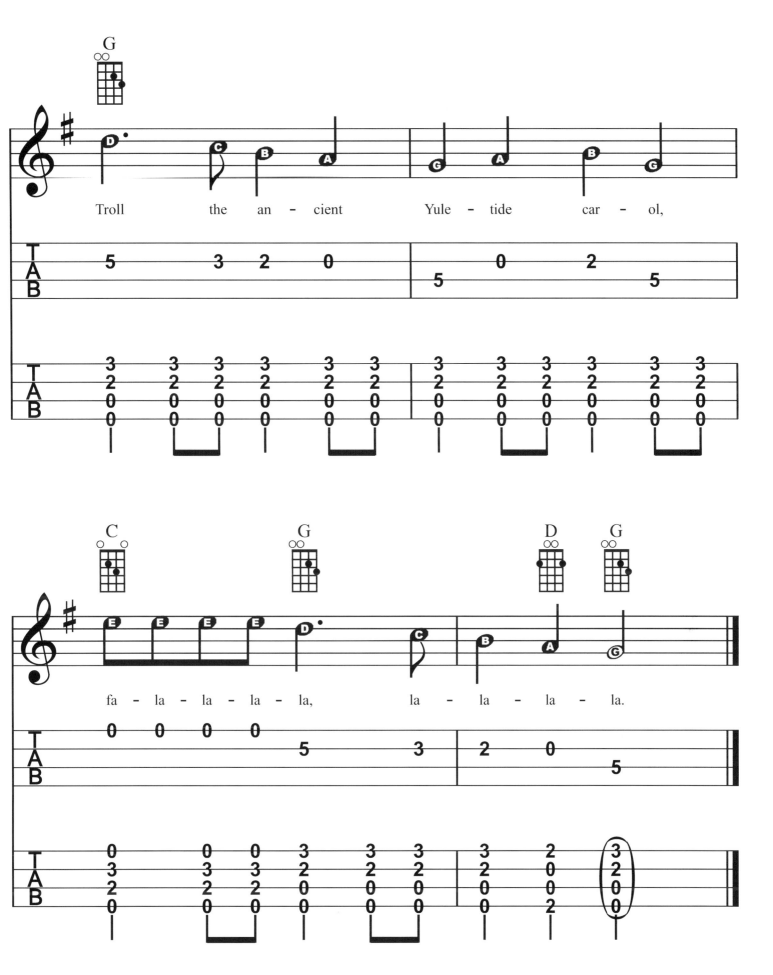

GO TELL IT ON THE MOUNTAIN

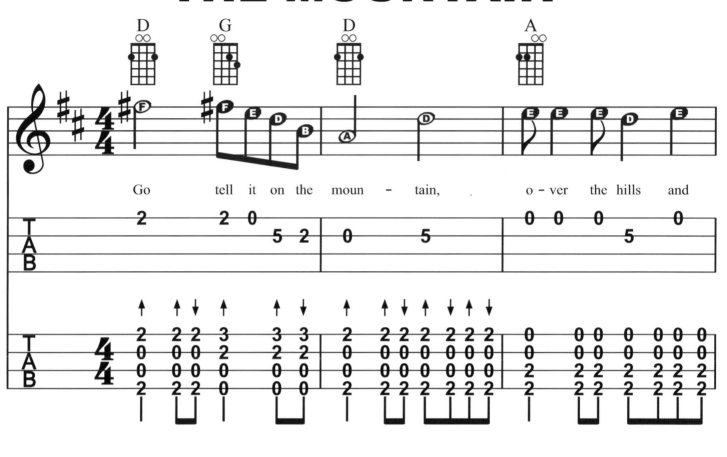

Go tell it on the moun - tain, o - ver the hills and

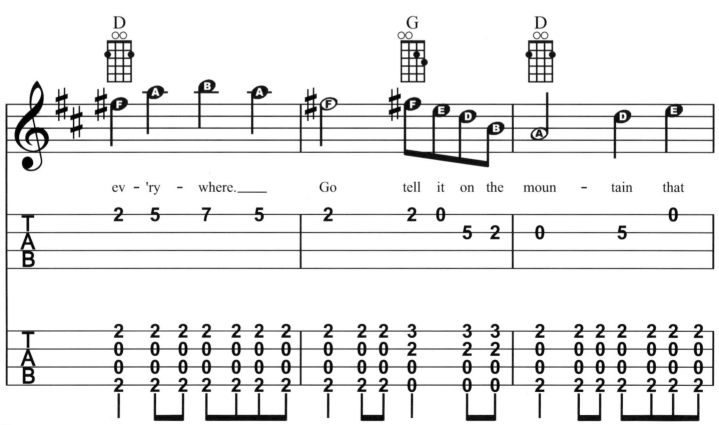

ev - 'ry - where.____ Go tell it on the moun - tain that

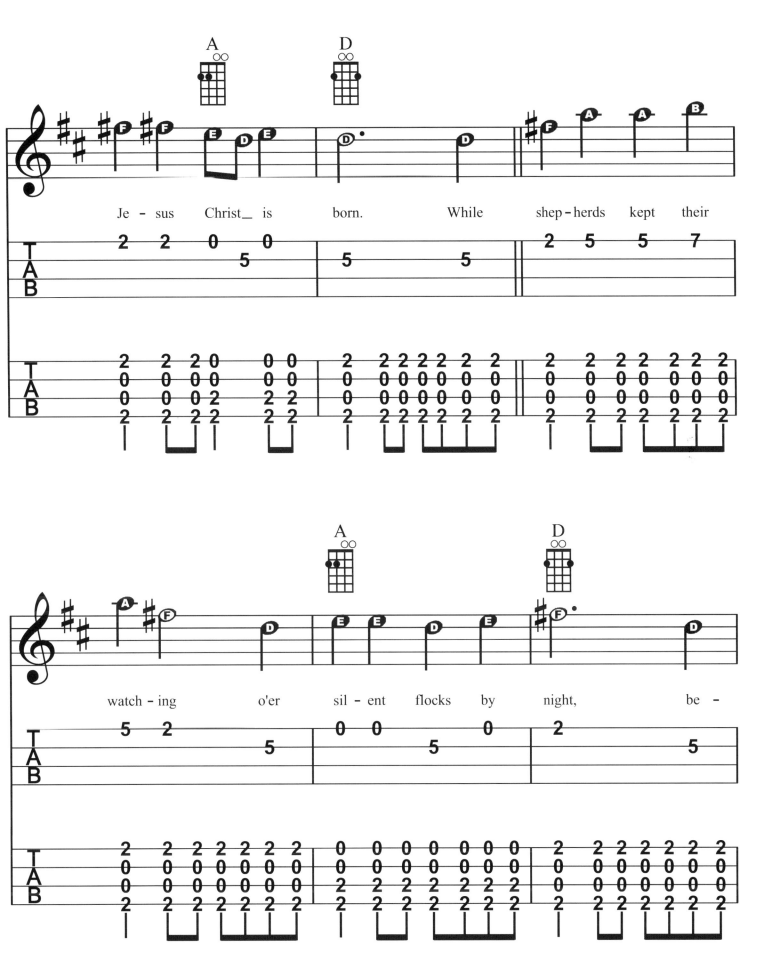

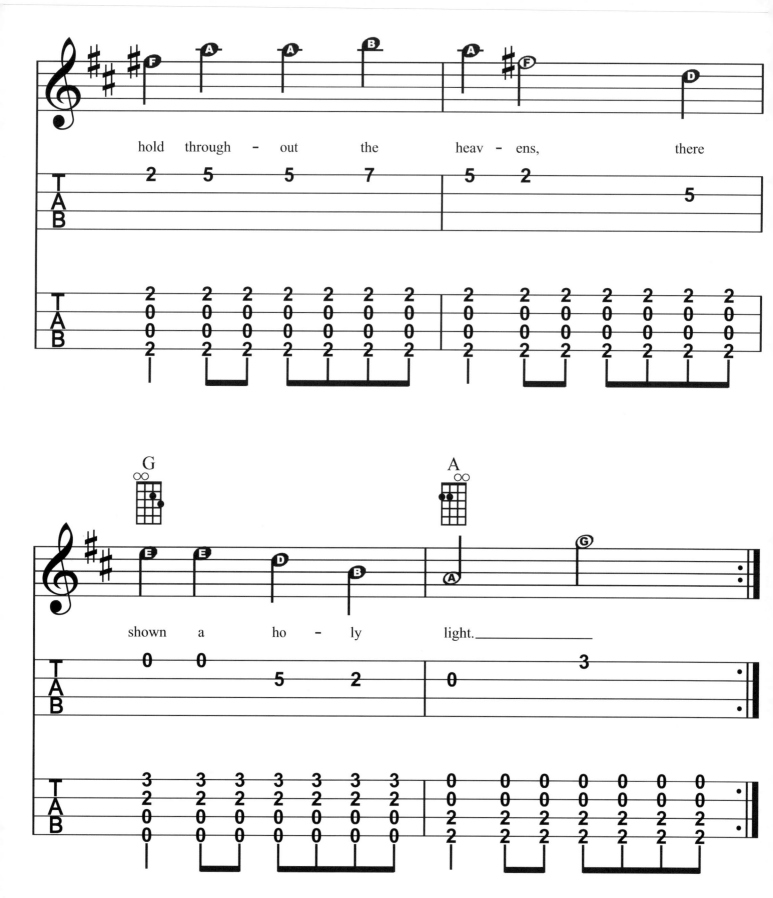

GOD REST YE MERRY GENTLEMEN

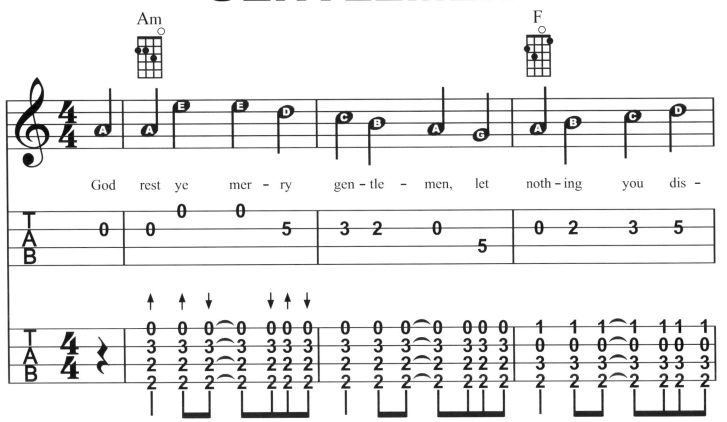

God rest ye mer – ry gen – tle – men, let noth – ing you dis –

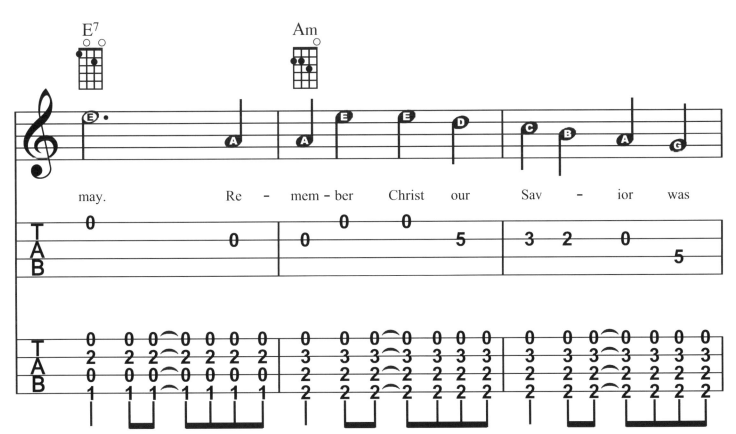

may. Re – mem – ber Christ our Sav – ior was

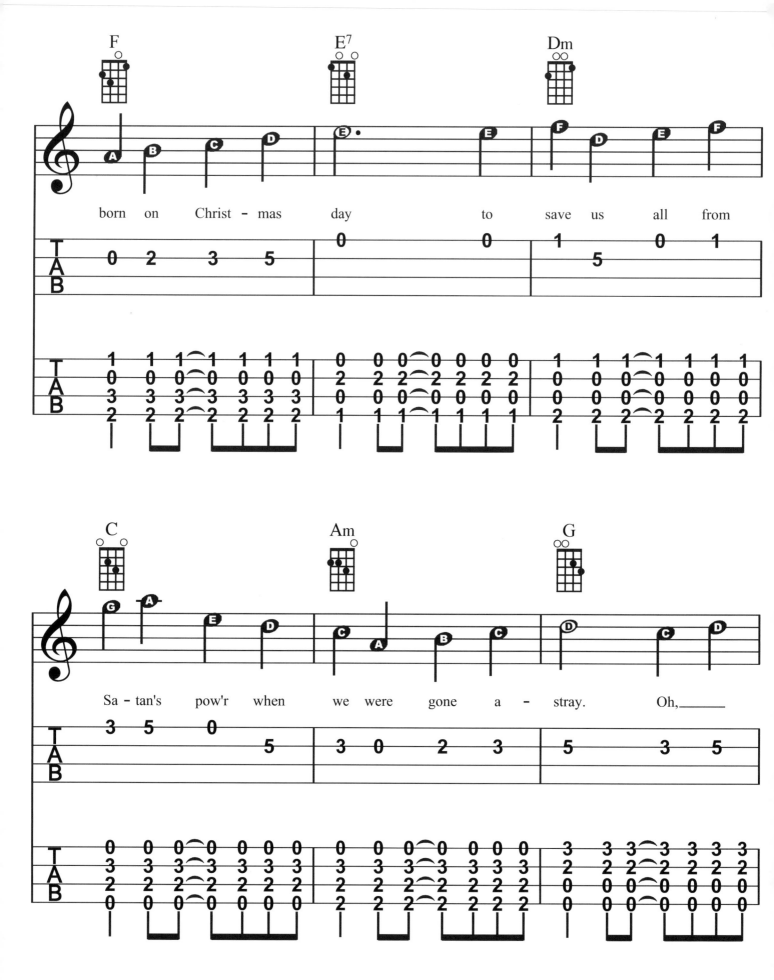

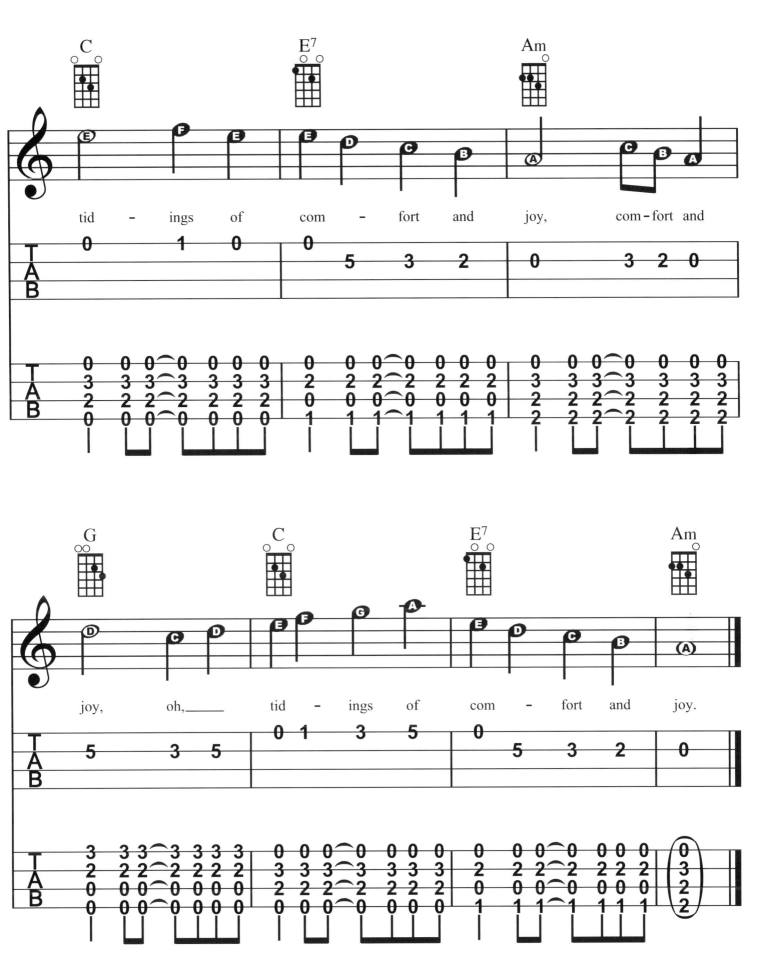

HARK! THE HERALD ANGELS SING

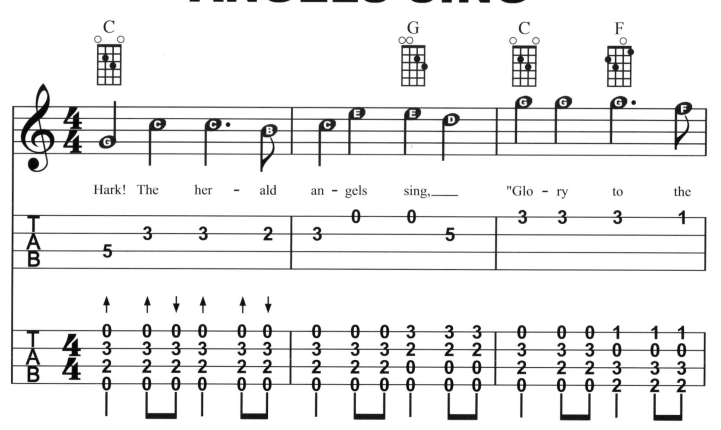

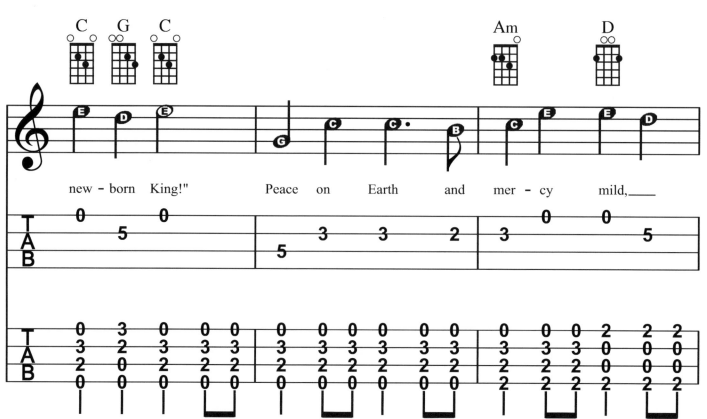

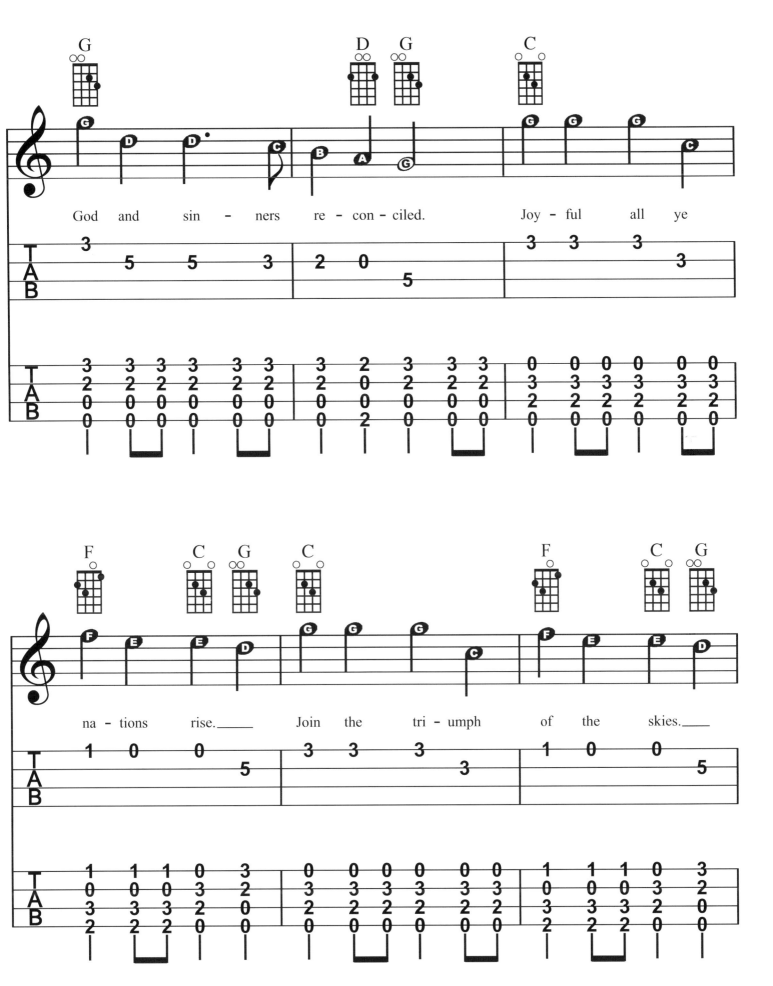

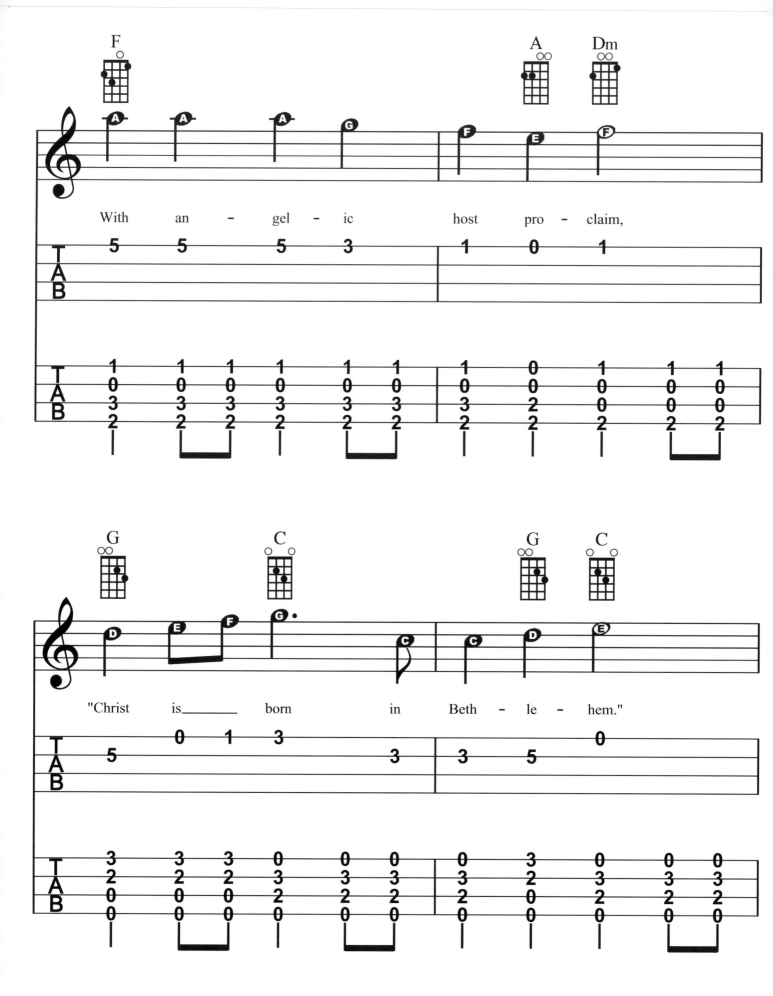

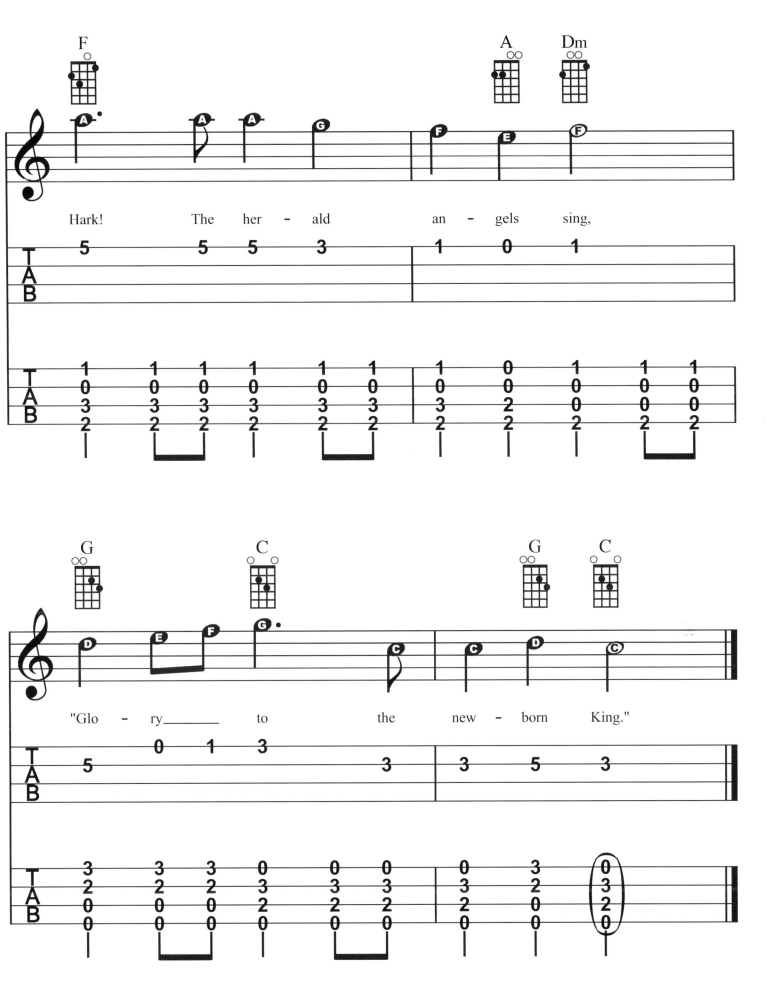

HERE WE COME A-CAROLING

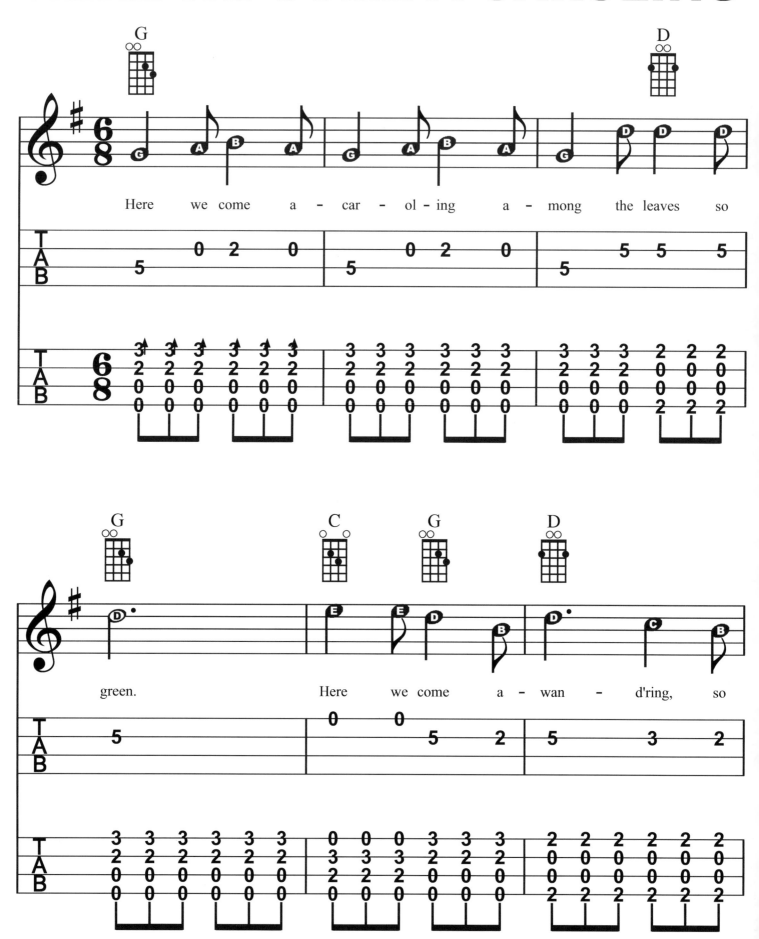

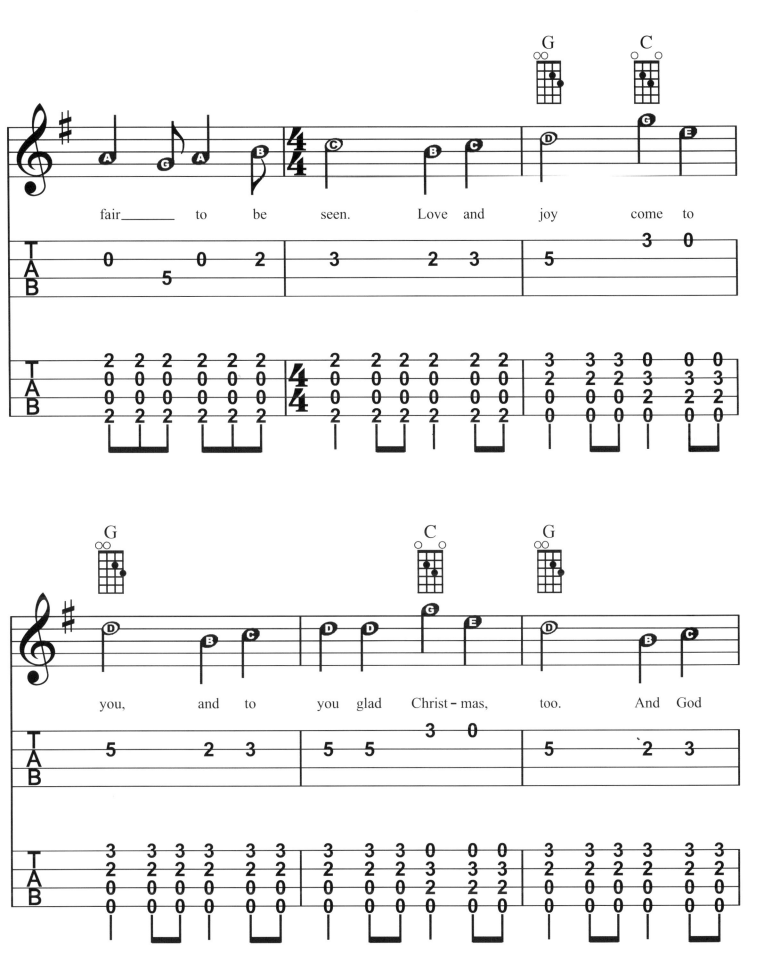

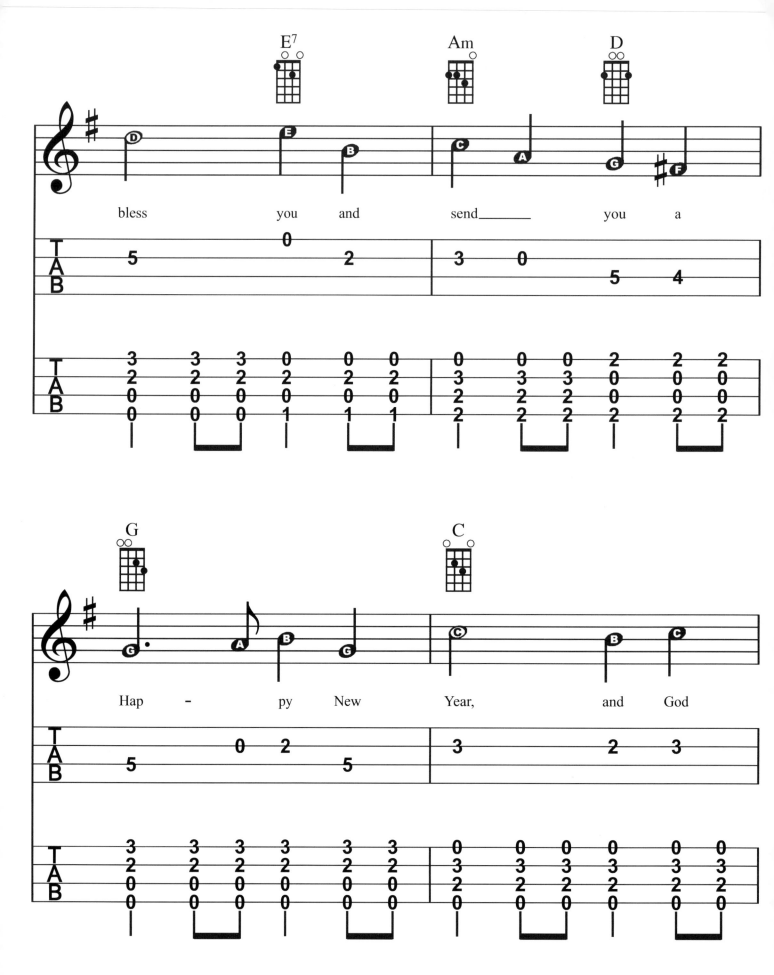

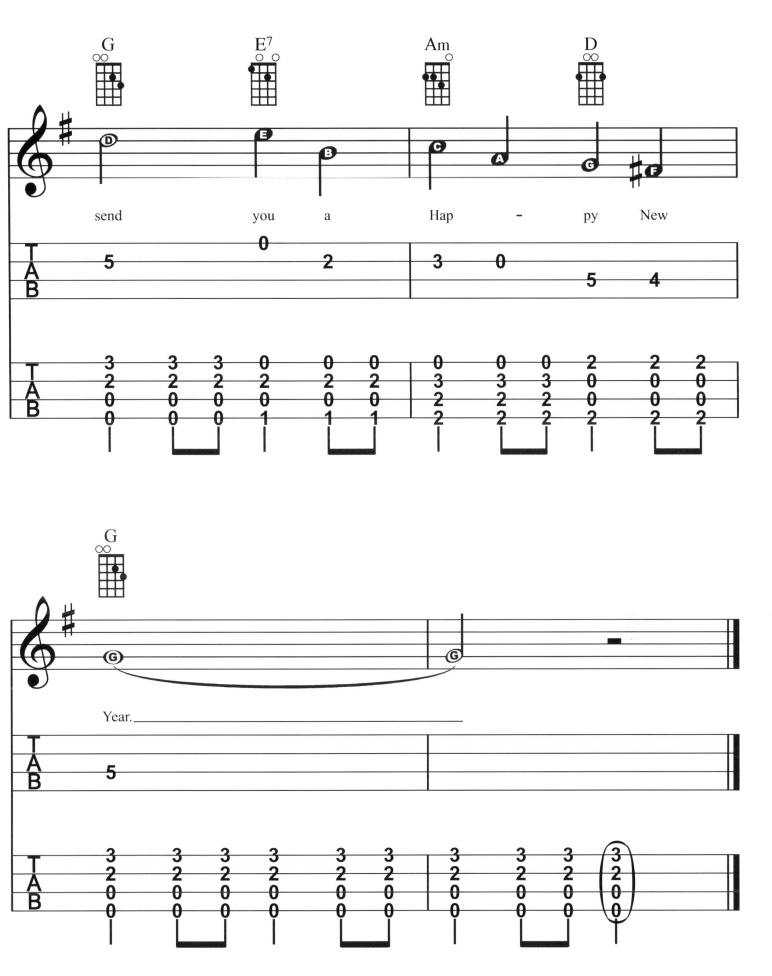

I SAW THREE SHIPS

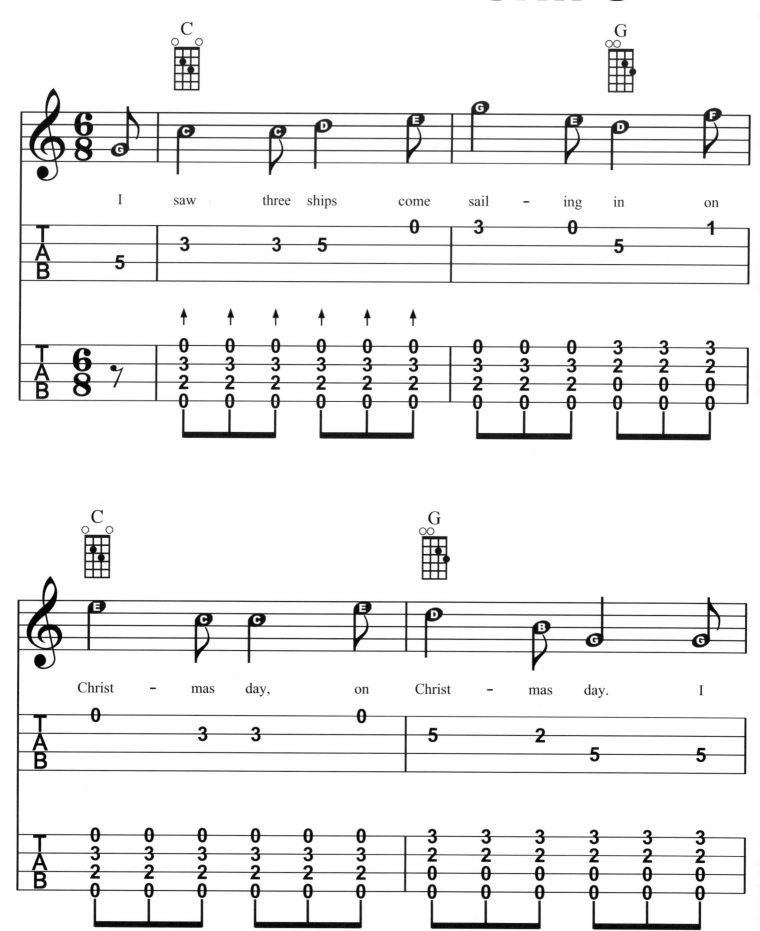

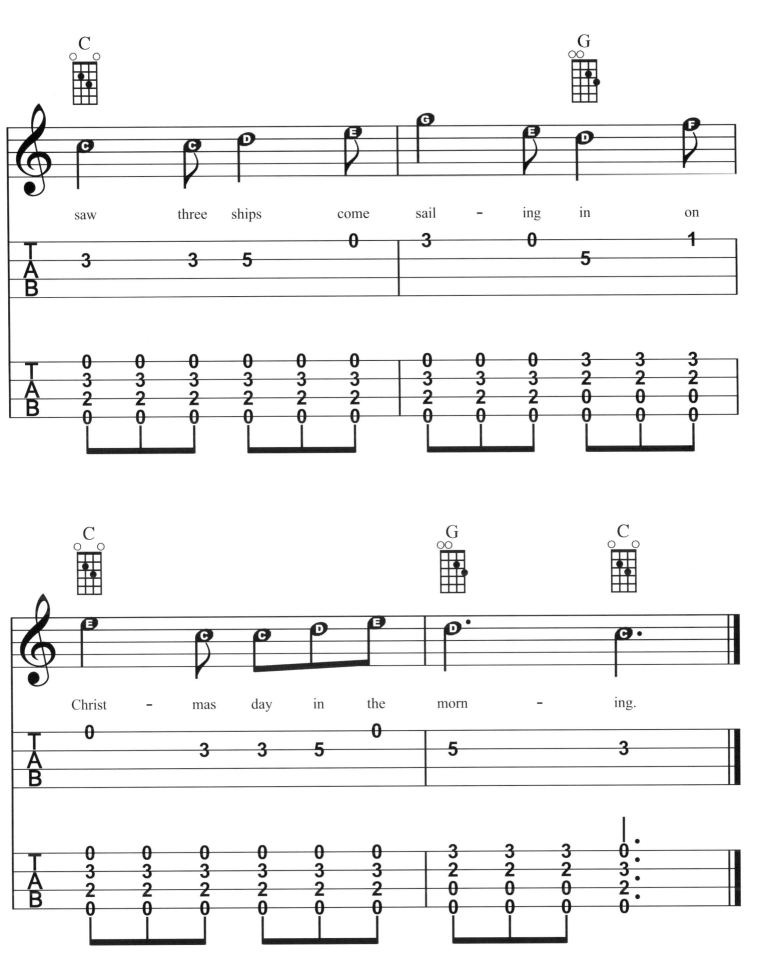

IT CAME UPON THE MIDNIGHT CLEAR

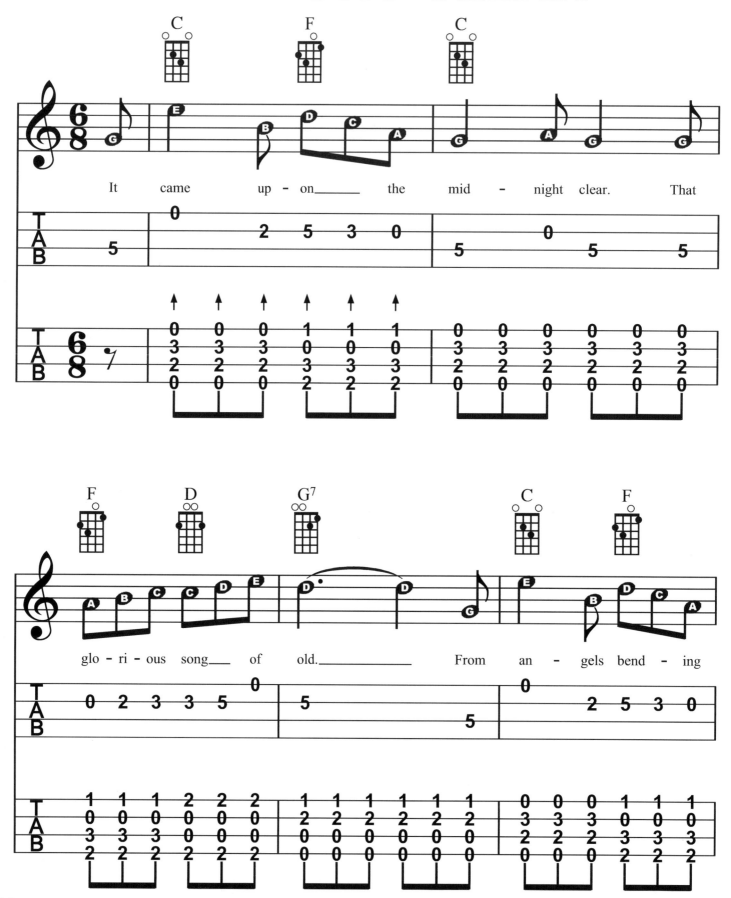

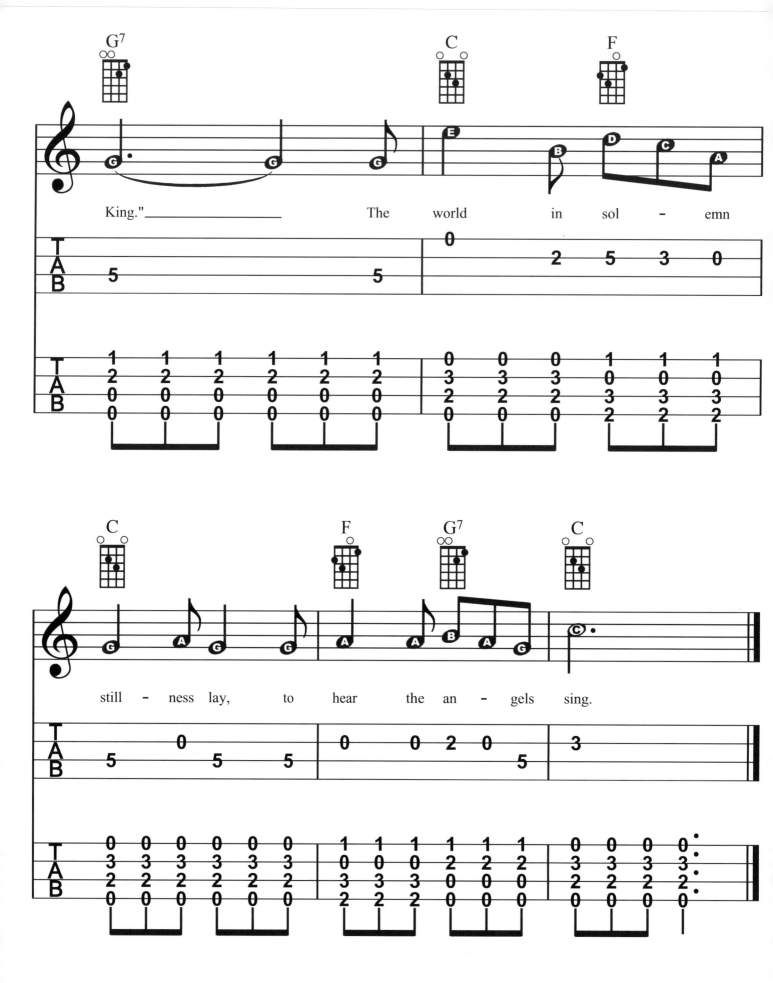

JINGLE BELLS

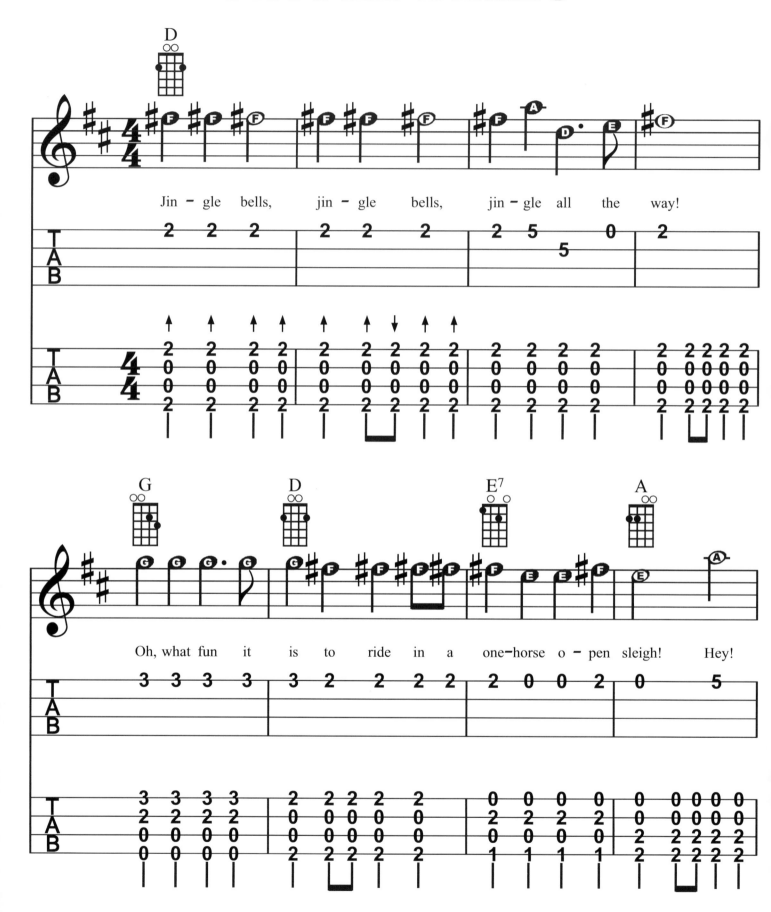

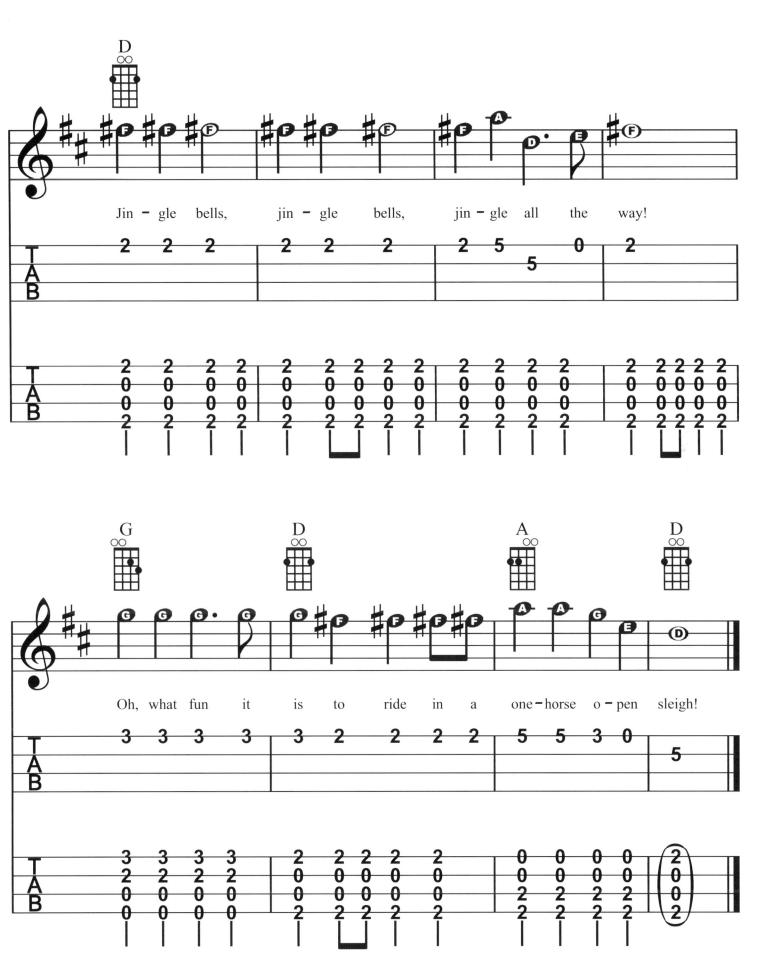

JOLLY OLD ST. NICHOLAS

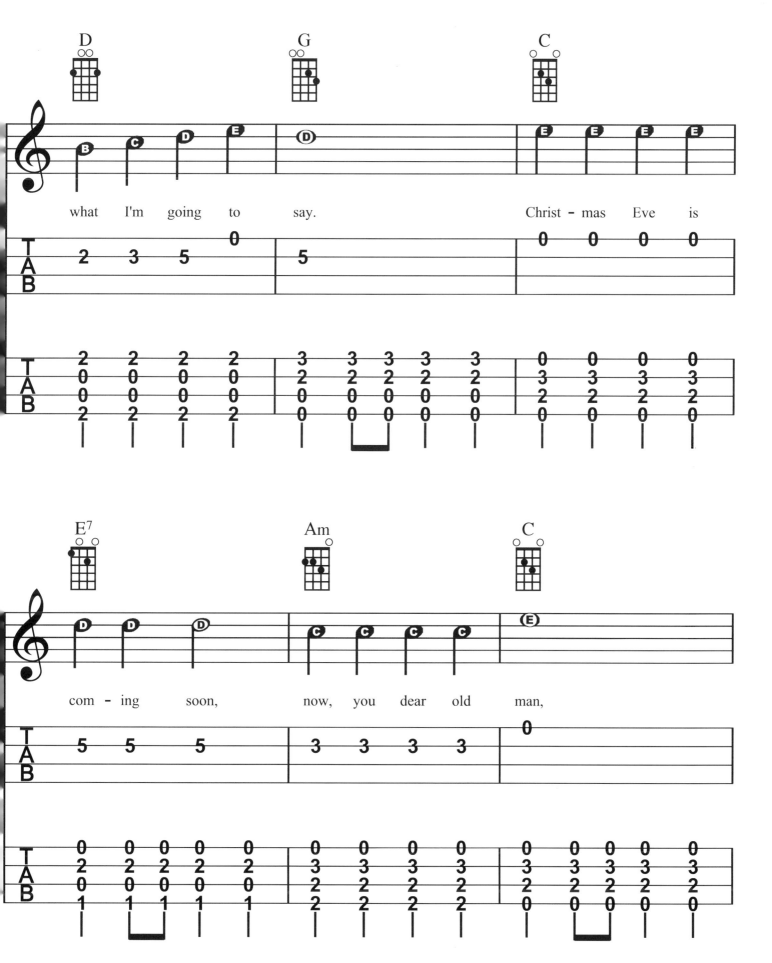

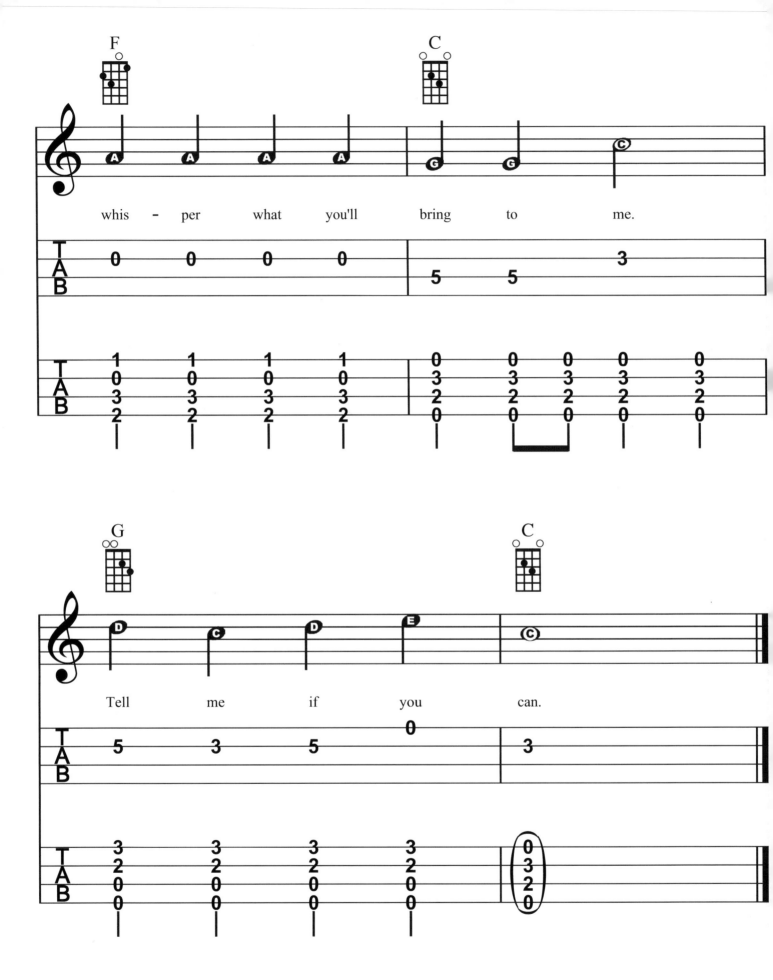

JOY TO THE WORLD

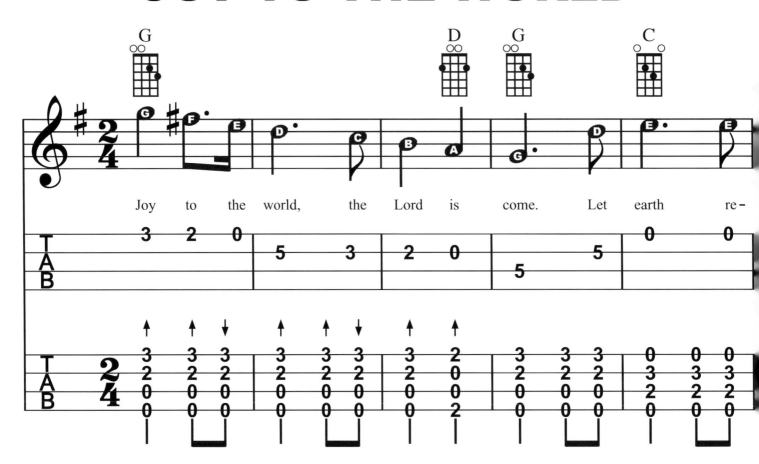

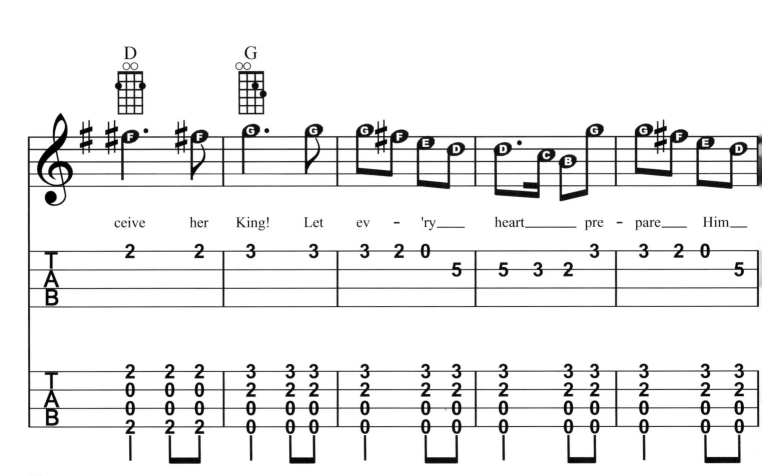

O CHRISTMAS TREE

O COME, ALL YE FAITHFUL

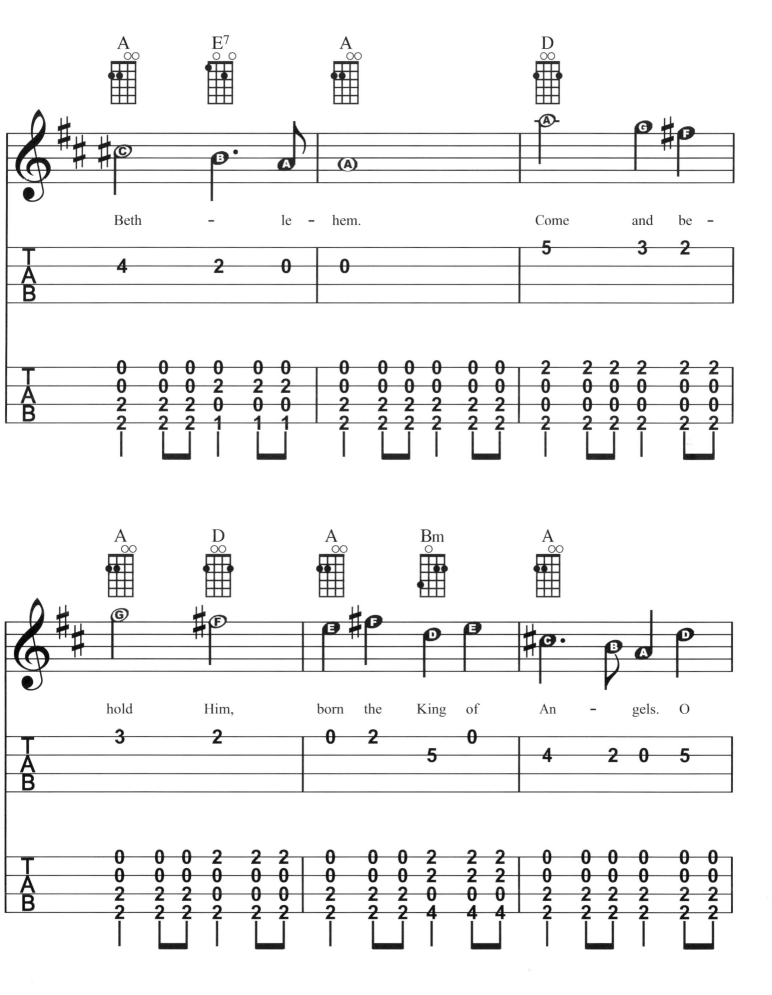

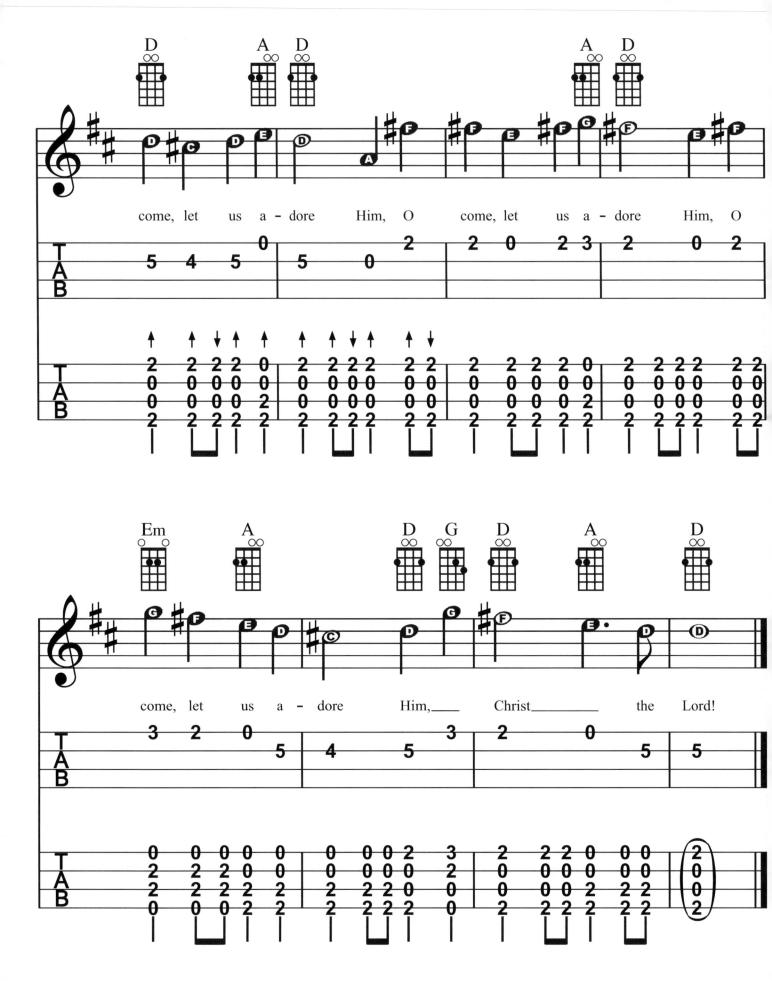

O COME, O COME EMMANUEL

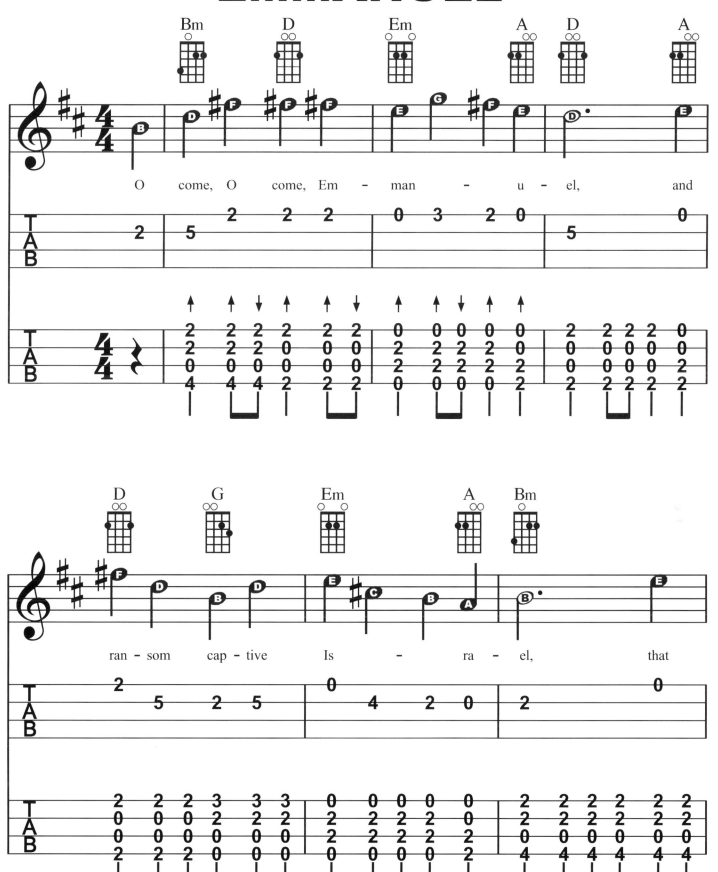

mourns in lone-ly ex - ile here, un-

til the Son of God_____ ap - pears. Re -

O LITTLE TOWN OF BETHLEHEM

O lit - tle town of Beth - le - hem, how still we___ see thee lie! A - bove thy deep and dream - less sleep the

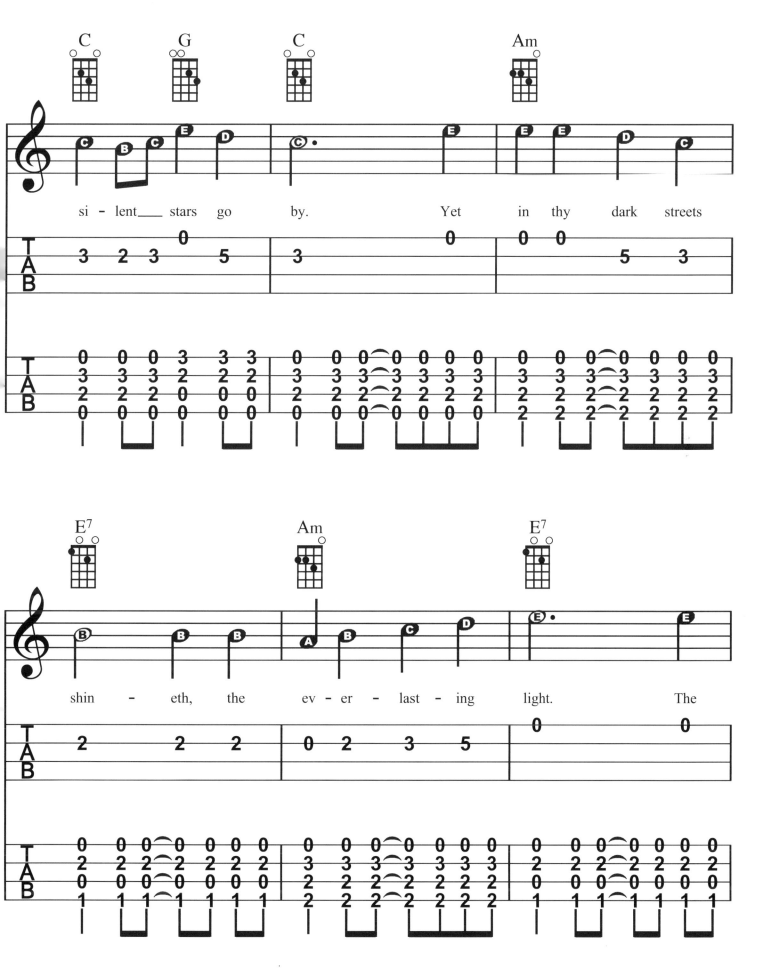

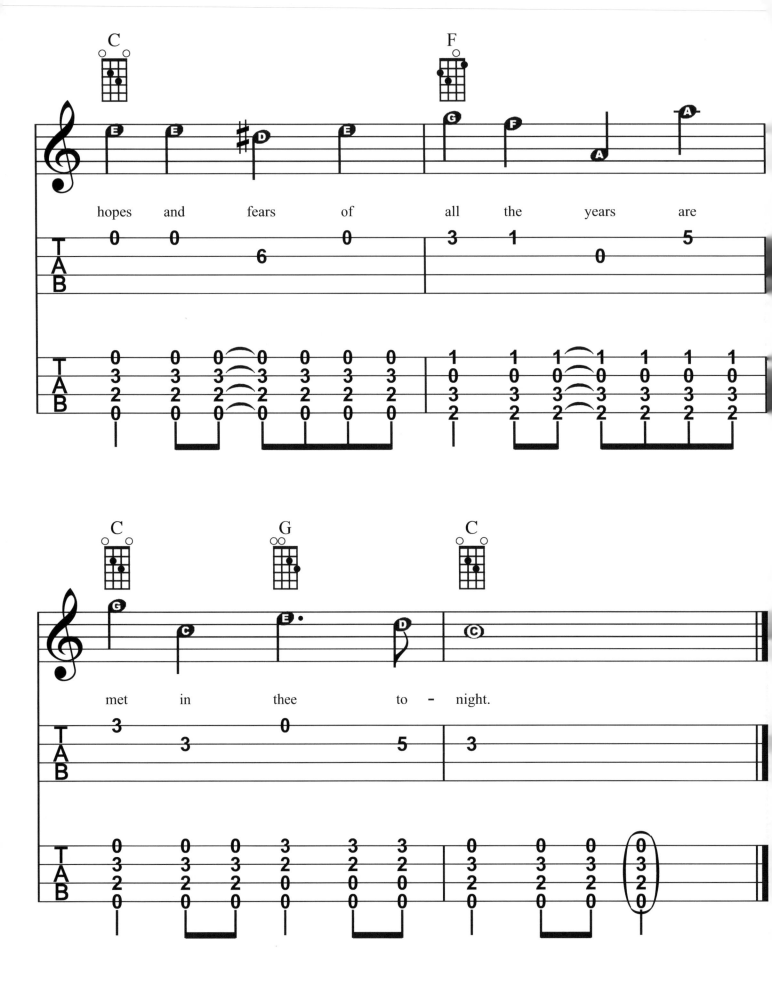

OVER THE RIVER AND THROUGH THE WOODS

horse knows the way to car - ry the sleigh through

white and drift - ing snow!

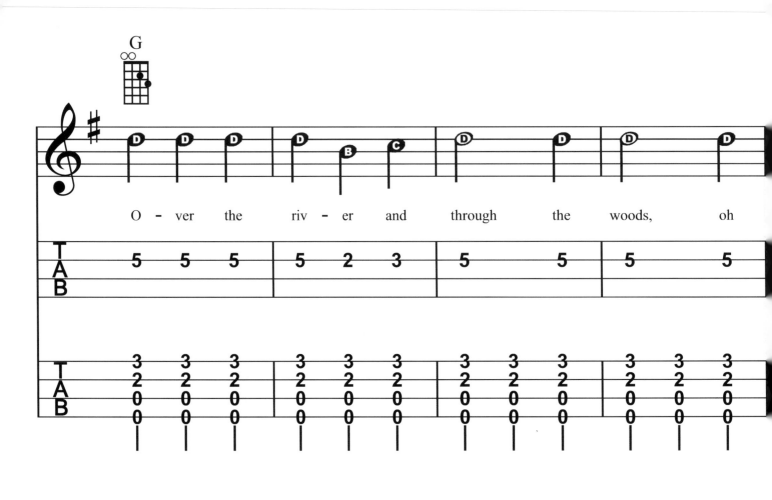

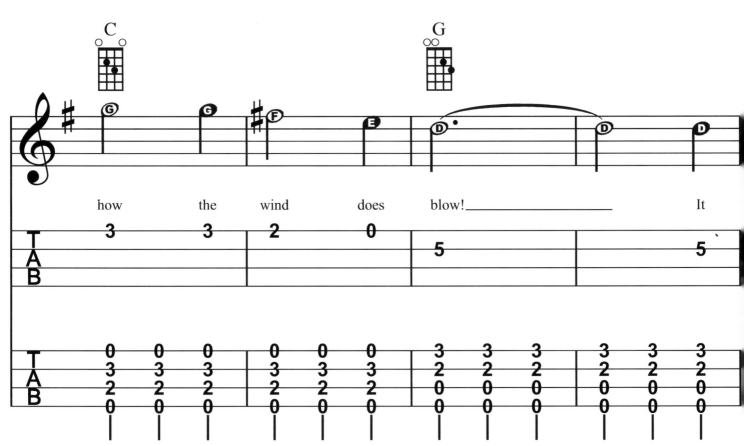

SILENT NIGHT

Si - lent night,   Ho - ly night!

All   is   calm,   all   is   bright.

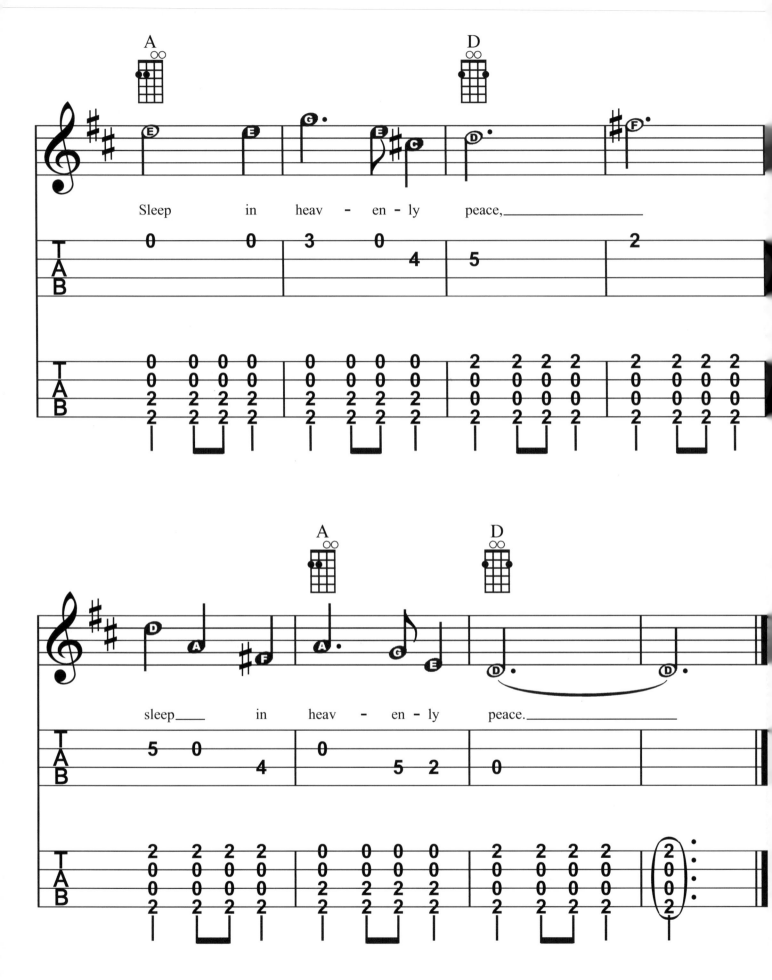

THE FIRST NOEL

UP ON THE HOUSETOP

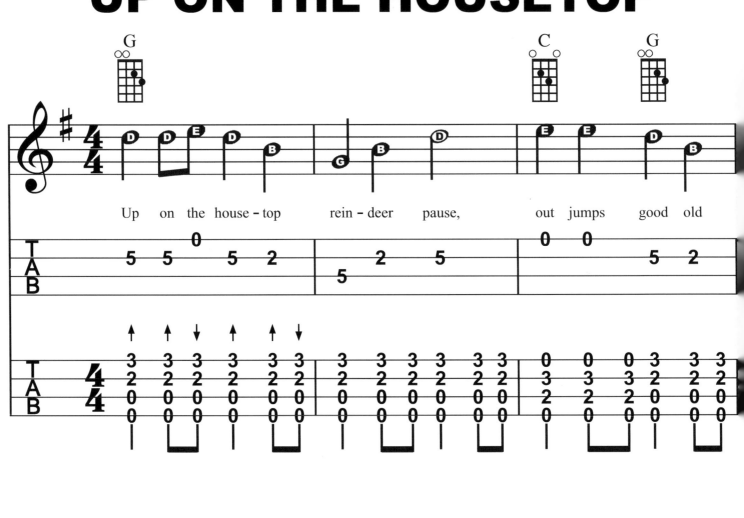

Up on the house-top rein-deer pause, out jumps good old

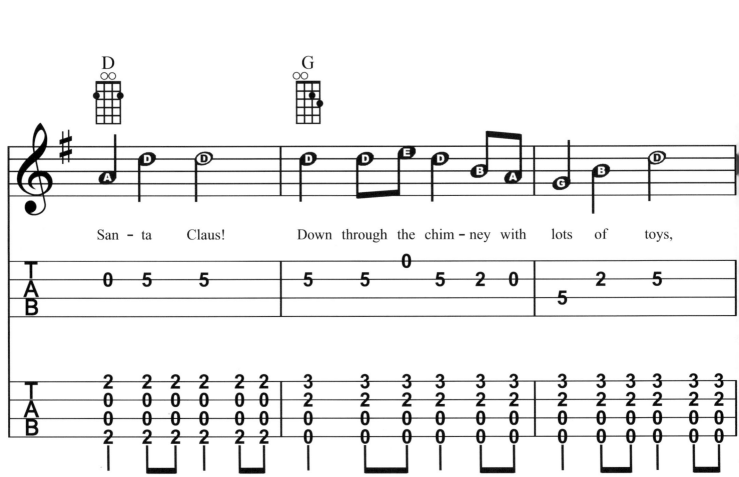

San-ta Claus! Down through the chim-ney with lots of toys,

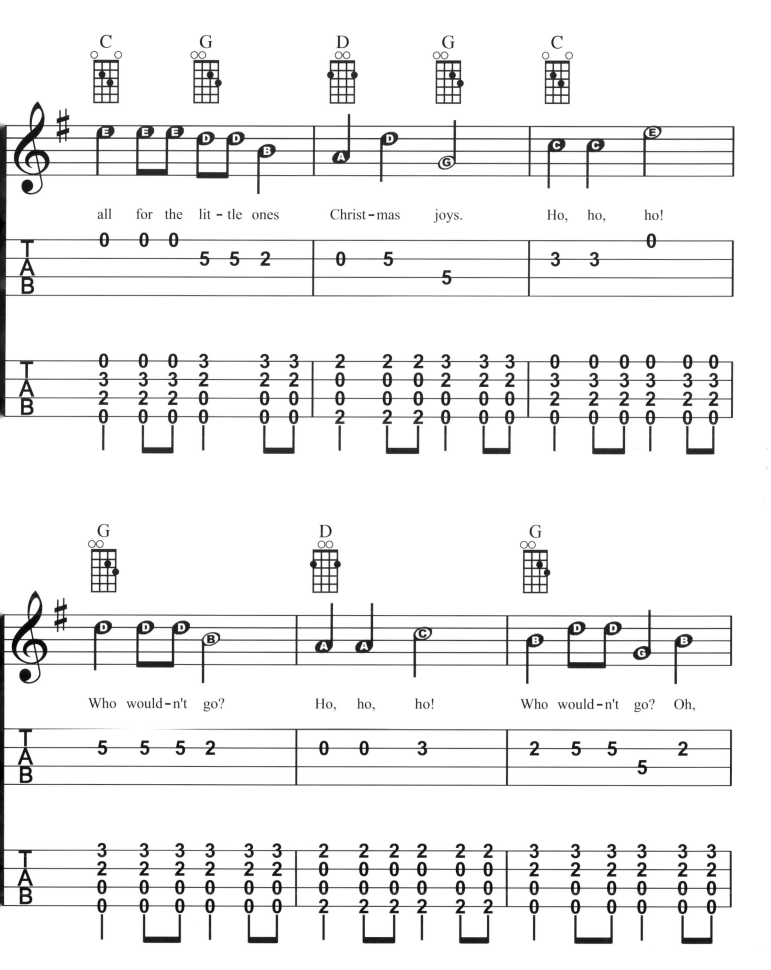

WE THREE KINGS

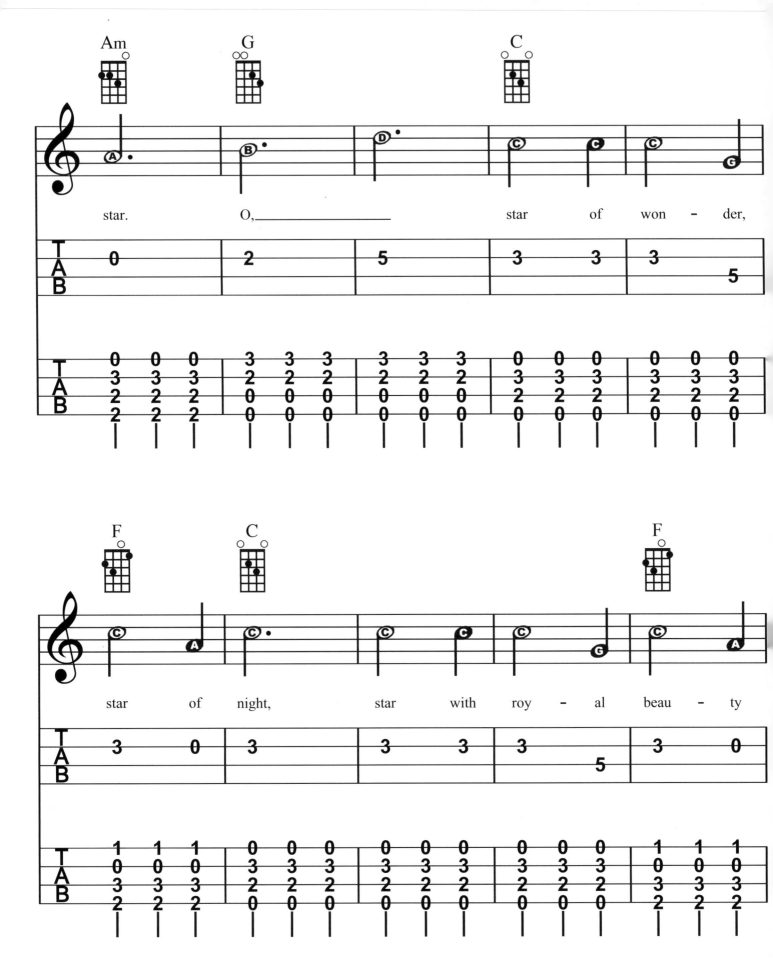

WE WISH YOU A MERRY CHRISTMAS

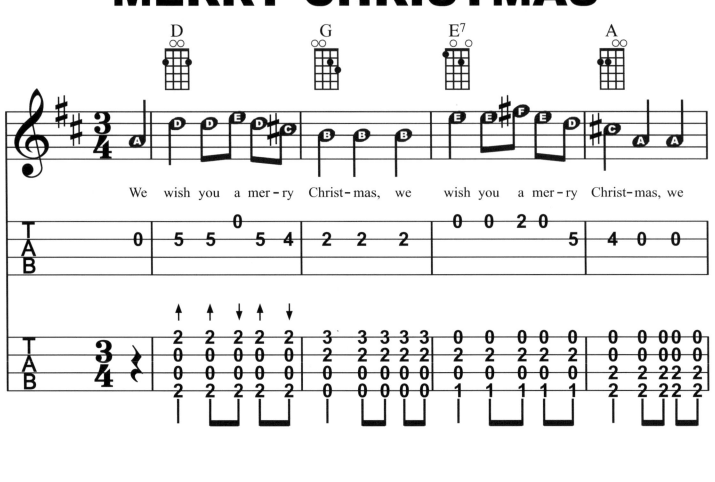

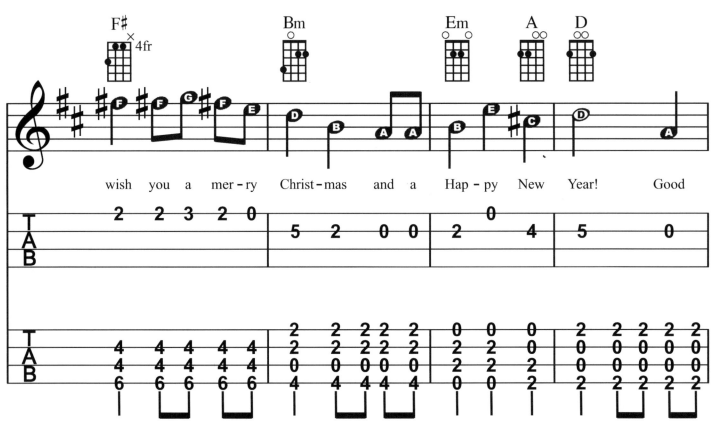

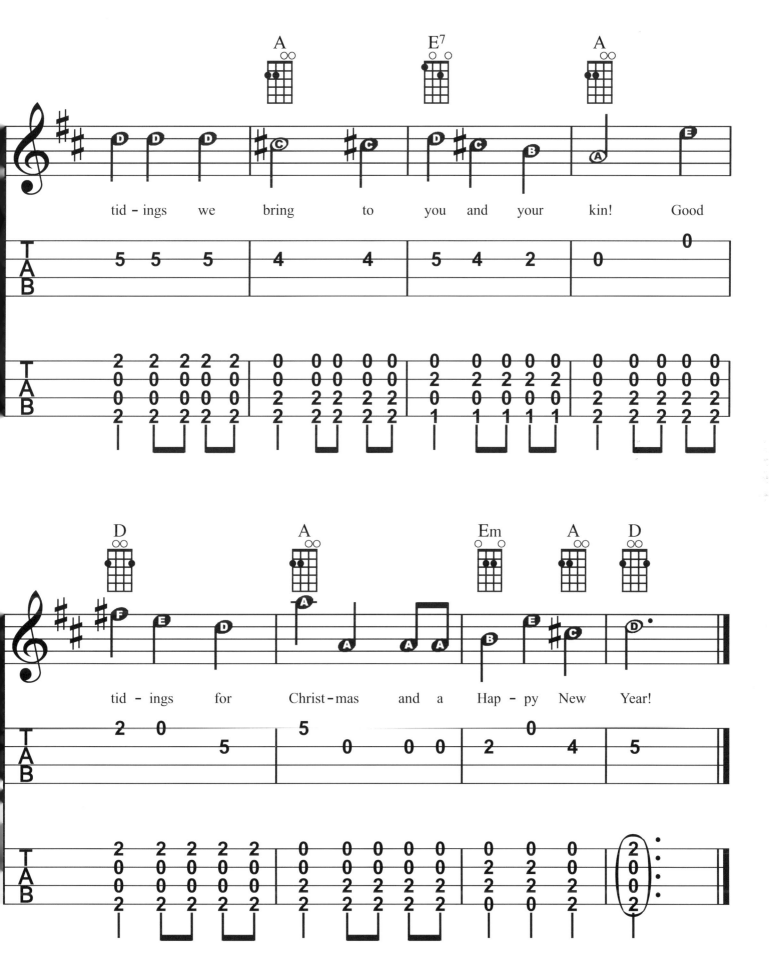

WHAT CHILD IS THIS

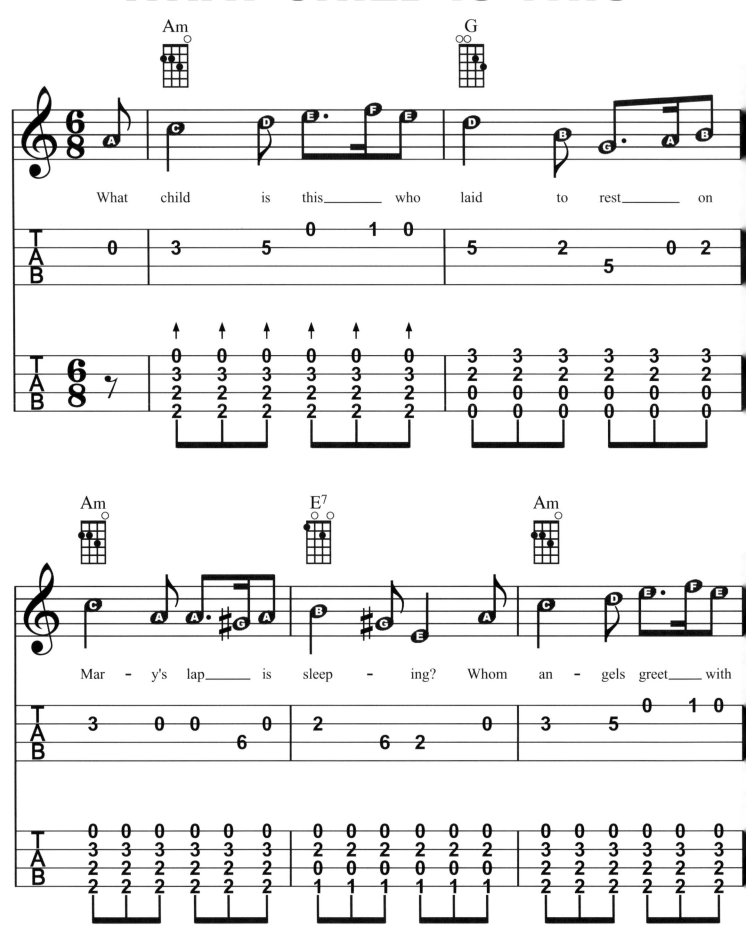

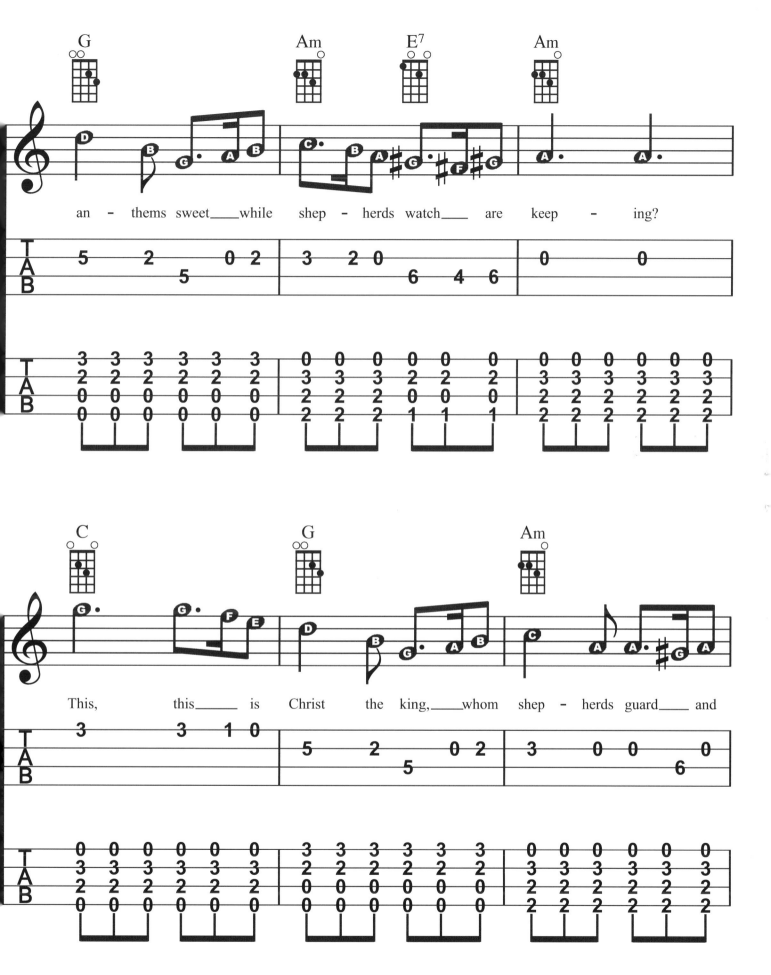

Printed in Great Britain
by Amazon

36572663R00046